Dog Heroes

THERAPY DOGS

WITHDRAWN

by Linda Tagliaferro

Consultant: Wilma Melville, Founder
National Disaster Search Dog Foundation

BEARPORT
PUBLISHING COMPANY, INC.

New York, New York

Special thanks to Wilma Melville who founded the:
National Disaster Search Dog Foundation
206 N. Signal Street, Suite R
Ojai, CA 93023
(888) 4K9-HERO
www.SearchDogFoundation.org

The Search Dog Foundation is a not-for-profit organization that rescues dogs, gives them professional training, and partners them with firefighters to find people buried alive in disasters. They produce the most highly trained search dogs in the nation.

The author would like to thank the following people for their generous help with the research for this book: Dr. Alan Beck of the Purdue University School of Veterinary Medicine, Dianne Bell of the Delta Society's Pet Partners program, Michelle Cobey of the Delta Society, Julie Diamond of Canine Companions for Independence, Dr. Aubrey Fine of California State Polytechnic University, Rachel Friedman of the North Star Foundation, Joy Hardaker of Ronald McDonald House in Jacksonville, Florida, Nancy Lind of Rainbow Assisted Animal Therapy, Marcy and Richard Lowy of HOPE Animal Assisted Crisis Response, and Jorjan Powers and Nancy Pierson of the Assistance Dog Institute.

Design and production by Dawn Beard Creative and Octavo Design and Production, Inc.

Credits

Cover Photos: Front (left), AP / Wide World Photos; (top right), Canine Companions for Independence, (center right), Elena Rooraid / Photo Edit, (bottom right), Canine Companions for Independence; Back (top), Canine Companions for Independence, (center), Elena Rooraid / Photo Edit, (bottom), Canine Companions for Independence. Title page, AP / Wide World Photos. Page 3, Elena Rooraid / Photo Edit; 4-5, Sandii McDonald / Alamy; 5, Elena Rooraid / Photo Edit; 6, Frank Pedrick / Index Stock; 7, Jacky Chapman, Janine Wiedel Photolibrary / Alamy; 8-9 (both), AP / Wide World Photos; 10-11, Archivo Iconografico, S.A. / CORBIS; 11, Frank Pedrick / Index Stock; 12, David Young-Wolff / Alamy; 12-13, Juniors Bildarchiv Alamy; 14, Canine Companions for Independence; 14-15, Ronnie Kaufman / CORBIS; 16-17, Jerry Arcieri / CORBIS;17, Harald Theissen / imagebroker / Alamy; 18, Canine Companions for Independence;19, Mario Tama / Getty Images; 20, 21, Canine Companions for Independence; 22-23, Canine Companions for Independence; 23, courtesy, Joy Hardaker / Ronald McDonald House of Jacksonville, Inc.; 24-25, CORBIS; 25, Ira Wyman / CORBIS SYGMA; 26-27(both), AP / Wide World Photos; 28, Sonda Dawes / The Image Works; 29(both), Photodisc / Fotosearch.

Library of Congress Cataloging-in-Publication Data

Tagliaferro, Linda.
Therapy dogs / by Linda Tagliaferro; consultant, Wilma Melville
    p. cm.—(Dog heroes)
Includes bibliographical references and index.
ISBN 1-59716-018-0 (lib. bdg.)—ISBN 1-59716-041-5 (pbk.)
1. Dogs—Therapeutic use—Juvenile literature. I. Melville, Wilma. II. Title. III. Series.

RM931.D63T34 2005
636.7'0886—dc22

2004020754

For more information, write to Bearport Publishing Company, Inc., 101 Fifth Avenue, Suite 6R, New York, New York 10003. Printed in the United States of America.

3 4 5 6 7 8 9 10

Table of Contents

Kisses from a Furry Friend

The little boy had **autism**, which made it hard for him to deal with change. When his dad left for the army, the boy became very sad. He couldn't sleep well. He sat alone in his room for hours at a time.

One day, however, something wonderful happened. His mom brought home a special dog. When she opened the door to their house, the animal ran inside. Right away, the dog found the boy and licked his face. For the first time since his dad left, the boy smiled.

People in pain sometimes need less medicine after they play with a therapy dog.

Helping People

The boy's new friend was a **therapy** dog. He had been trained to cheer up people who are sad, lonely, or sick. Therapy dogs visit people in homes, hospitals, and schools. When people see a friendly dog, they often forget that they don't feel well.

A therapy dog visits a sick man in the hospital.

Therapy dogs may work with a group of people or with just one person. Sometimes, they visit people who can't keep dogs where they live. Many therapy animals, however, live with the people who need their help.

This therapy dog keeps his owner company.

Petting a dog can cause a person's heart to beat more slowly. A slower heartbeat means that the person is calm.

Spreading Cheer

Some therapy dogs live with healthy people who want their animals to help others. These people enjoy seeing their dogs cheer up sick children and adults in hospitals and other places.

Working with a therapy dog puts a smile on Nat Little's face.

Other therapy dogs help people after **disasters**. In 1995, a building in Oklahoma City, Oklahoma, was blown up. Many therapy dogs helped people who lost loved ones. After a disaster happens, therapy dogs can be there to help in a few hours.

Sarah Ferguson, the Duchess of York, and P.J. Allen, who was hurt in the Oklahoma City bombing, with a therapy dog

When people are upset, they give off a special smell. Some therapy dogs can sniff out this smell.

9

The Beginning

In the late 1700s in England, a country in Europe, dogs helped make sick people feel better. They visited hospitals for people who had problems with their minds. The animals calmed down the **patients**. They helped them forget about the things that made them sad or angry.

In the 1960s, Boris Levinson came up with the name "pet therapy" for this kind of work. He was an American doctor who helped people deal with their feelings. Today, tens of thousands of therapy dogs work in the United States.

A dog visits with a patient at a hospital.

In the 1800s, Florence Nightingale, a nurse, used her pet owl as a therapy animal.

Even as early as the 15th century, people and dogs worked together.

Love in All Sizes

Almost any **breed** of dog can become a therapy dog. Big animals, such as German shepherds and Labrador retrievers, can put a smile on a person's face. Small dogs, such as Yorkshire terriers and Chihuahuas, can sit on people's laps. All therapy dogs, big or small, understand how to be kind to the people they meet.

Small dogs, such as this Chihuahua, make great therapy dogs.

Therapy dogs sometimes help calm down people who were hurt in a crime.

The best therapy dogs are friendly and well-behaved. They are quiet and calm. These animals enjoy going to new places. They are used to people coming close to pet them.

Only the Best

Some people want their puppies to become therapy dogs from the time the animals are born. Animal doctors at a therapy dog training school check the puppies. The doctors make sure they are healthy. Then the little ones go to live with puppy raisers for one year. These people teach them simple **commands** like "sit" and "come."

Therapy dogs have to be comfortable around people in wheelchairs.

Frank Barnwell and a therapy dog at the Meadowlark Hills Retirement Community

When they are one year old, the puppies return to the training school. There, they spend a year learning special skills. Dogs that will work in hospitals learn to be calm around the special machines found there.

Therapy dogs sometimes help older people feel less lonely.

Preparing Pets

Sometimes a dog begins life as a pet. Later, the owner decides that the animal could help others. Together, they go to a dog therapy training school. There, the owner learns how to teach the pet important lessons. For example, the dog learns to stay calm around people and not to growl at noisy children.

When the training is finished, the owner and pet take a test. If they pass, they can visit places most dogs may not go, such as **nursing homes**.

Some therapy dogs work in prisons. They help the people there learn love and kindness.

The Big Day

On **graduation** day, the dogs and their owners meet at the school. Puppy raisers may also come to the school. They will hand over the leash of the dog they raised to the animal's new owner.

At graduation, the dogs might be given a **badge** or a cape. The animals wear this gift when they work in a hospital, school, or nursing home. It lets people know that they are well trained and have come to help.

People started keeping dogs as pets about 14,000 years ago.

Gentle Ben (the black dog in the middle) received a medal in 2004 for his therapy work in hospitals.

Dogs that Work in Schools

Many therapy dogs work in schools with children who have **physical** problems or trouble dealing with their feelings. Ozzie goes to school with his **partner** Lee, who is the head of the school. There, Ozzie plays with the children. Some of the children had trouble learning to talk. Now that Ozzie comes around, they can speak in whole sentences.

Ozzie plays with children in a classroom.

Star goes to a special school with her partner Judith. Once a week, the children sit on the floor and read aloud. Star lies on the floor and listens quietly. The children learn to read better when Star comes to class.

Judith and Star reading with students

Rabbits, cats, and even chickens are used as therapy animals.

Helping to Heal

Therapy dogs help people's bodies heal, too. Ty works with Claudia, a physical therapist. One of Claudia's patients has a hard time moving her left arm. Playing games of tug with Ty, however, makes her arm stronger.

Anita helps people heal in a different way. She and her human partner Joy visit the Ronald McDonald House in Florida. Families stay there when their sick children need to visit doctors in the area. Anita makes the children laugh when she does tricks like jumping though a hoop.

Anita and Joy

People breathe more slowly when therapy dogs are around because the dogs help them relax.

Safety on the Job

The partners of therapy dogs make sure their animals stay safe at work. In hospitals, they check the floors for spills. They make sure the dog doesn't pick up food or medicine that has fallen.

The partner also makes sure the dog is clean. He washes and brushes the dog's coat. He clips the dog's nails so they don't scratch people. Sometimes the partner brushes the dog's teeth and gives him breath spray.

It's important for partners to make sure their therapy dogs stay clean.

Sweating helps people cool off when they get hot. Dogs, however, don't sweat as much as people. Dogs need lots of water to keep cool when working in warm places.

Willing Workers

Scientists are studying the ways dogs help people stay happy and healthy. They know that people with heart problems, for example, generally live longer if they have a dog. Perhaps these people stay healthier because their faithful friends make them feel happier.

Bradley Kooken reads with therapy dog, Danny Boy, at the Leesburg Public Library in Florida.

Some people are studying robot dogs. They hope these dogs will cheer up people who are too sick to raise a real dog.

Therapy dogs enjoy their jobs. They live with people who love them, and they get to meet new people all the time. Their tails wag and their eyes shine as they work with the people who need them most.

Brian reads to his classmate Tyler. Therapy dog Buster and his partner Joan help out.

Just the Facts

- Therapy dogs sit up and "shake paws" with sad people to make them laugh.

- Therapy dogs can be male or female.

- Many therapy dogs work for 8 to 10 years.

- One out of three people in the United States owns a dog.

- Children as young as 10 years old can go along when their parents take therapy dogs on visits.

- Therapists help people deal with their feelings. Some therapists bring therapy dogs to the office to make patients feel safe.

All breeds of dogs, large or small, can work as therapy dogs.

Boston terrier

Labrador retriever

autism (AW-tiz-uhm) a condition that causes people to have trouble communicating with and relating to others

badge (BAJ) a small sign with a picture or message that you can pin to your clothes

breed (BREED) type of a certain animal

commands (kuh-MANDZ) instructions to be obeyed; orders

disasters (duh-ZASS-turz) sudden events causing much damage, loss, or suffering

graduation (GRAJ-oo-*ay*-shuhn) the time when someone finishes a course of study in a school

nursing homes (NUR-sing HOMEZ) places that provide a home and nursing care for people who are old or ill

partner (PART-nur) one of two or more people who do something together

patients (PAY-shuhnts) people who are getting treatment from a doctor

physical (FIZ-uh-kuhl) having to do with the body

robot (ROH-bot) a machine that can do jobs that a person or animal might do

therapy (THER-uh-pee) a treatment for an illness or injury

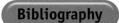
Bibliography

"Animal Assisted Therapy." http://dogs.about.com/cs/sportsrecreation/p/
animal_therapy.htm.

Bogle, Lara. "Therapy Dogs Seem to Boost Health of Sick and Lonely." *National Geographic News.* http://news.nationalgeographic.com/news/2002/08/
0808_020808_therapydogs.html (August 8, 2002).

Kane, Ed. "Animals Healing Children." http://www.deltasociety.org/petpart/
ppart0102.htm.

"Visiting Pets and Animal Assisted Therapy." http://www.dog-play.com/therapy.html.

"What Is TDI?" http://www.tdi-dog.org.

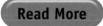
Read More

Calmenson, Stephanie, and Justin Sutcliffe. *Rosie: A Visiting Dog's Story.*
New York, NY: Clarion Books (1994).

Johnson, Sharon Kay. *Therapy Dog and Other Stories.* Frederick, MD:
PublishAmerica, Inc. (2003).

Luke, Melinda, and Marcy Dunn Ramsey. *Helping Paws: Dogs That Serve.*
New York, NY: Cartwheel Books (2002).

Vinocur, Terry. *Dogs Helping Kids with Feelings.* New York, NY: PowerKids Press
(1999).

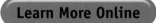
Learn More Online

Visit these Web sites to learn more about therapy dogs:

www.animalassistedcrisisresponse.org

www.assistancedog.org

www.cci.org

www.deltasociety.org/dsa000.htm

www.nctdinc.org

Index

About the Author

Linda Tagliaferro is an award-winning writer who lives in Little Neck, New York. This is her 16th book for children, and her third book about dogs. She has also written for adults and young adults.